CH00665563

A Senior Manager's Guide to Managing Benefits

Optimizing the return from investments

London: TSO

information & publishing solutions

Published by TSO (The Stationery Office)
and available from:

Online
www.tsoshop.co.uk

Mail, Telephone, Fax & E-mail
TSO
PO Box 29, Norwich, NR3 1GN
Telephone orders/General enquiries:
0870 600 5522
Fax orders: 0870 600 5533
E-mail: customer.services@tso.co.uk
Textphone 0870 240 3701

TSO@Blackwell and other Accredited Agents

APMG International
Sword House
Totteridge Road
High Wycombe
HP13 6DG

Contact: servicedesk@apmg-international.com
Web: www.apmg-international.com

Stephen Jenner has asserted his moral rights under the Copyright, Designs and Patents Act 1988 to be identified as the author of this work.

The APMG International Swirl Managing Benefits Device is a trade mark of APM Group Ltd

First edition © APMG-International 2012
Second edition 2015
ISBN 9780117082564

Contents

Foreword

Realizing benefits is the reason we invest in change. Would you hand over your hard-earned money for an investment if you were not confident of a positive return or that the potential return outweighed the risks involved? When we invest shareholders' and taxpayers' resources, it is our duty to ensure that there is a solid rationale for investment and that effective mechanisms are in place to optimize benefits realization in terms of:

- Increasing revenue
- Reducing costs
- Delivering a tangible contribution to a strategic objective or business priority
- Meeting a legal or regulatory requirement, or to maintain business as usual.

As such, benefits should be the driver behind all change initiatives from initiation through to and beyond implementation. Yet reports from professional bodies, audit agencies and academic research consistently show that organizations in the public, private and third sectors continue to struggle in demonstrating a return on their investments in change. The significance of this is even greater in the current economic climate, where this failure may put future initiatives at risk as investors lose confidence in the organization's ability to manage change effectively.

Benefits management, appropriately designed and applied, can address these issues by ensuring that we optimize the return from our investments in change – by ensuring that change initiatives are set up to succeed, based on realism in planning and enthusiasm in delivery, so that planned benefits are realized, unplanned benefits are fully exploited and the negative impacts of change are effectively mitigated.

This guide has been written specifically to provide senior managers with an overview of effective benefits management – the principles upon which it is based, its constituent practices, the techniques used and how you can get started and sustain progress.

I recommend it to you.

Alan Harpham
Chairman, APM Group

Acknowledgements

APMG International is grateful to the following for their contributions to the planning, design, authoring and review of this guide.

AUTHOR

Stephen Jenner is the author of both this and the companion practitioner guide, *Managing Benefits*™. He is also chief examiner for the accompanying accredited examinations from APMG International. Stephen has written several books in the field of benefits management and as a practitioner was responsible for the approach that won the Civil Service Financial Management award. This approach was also cited as good practice in reports to the OECD and European Commission (Cabinet Office, 2006). He is a professionally qualified management accountant and a fellow of the Association for Project Management (APM). He also holds an MBA and a Master of Studies degree from Cambridge University.

PROJECT MANAGER

James Davies   APMG International

REVIEWERS

The author and APMG International are happy to record their gratitude to the following reviewers of the draft of this guide.

Michael Acaster	Cabinet Office, Efficiency Reform Group
Jo Harper	Management consultant, Australia
Lex van der Helm	CapGemini Academy
Craig Kilford	Cansoti

Eileen Roden   Head of Project and Programme Management, QA Ltd

For more information about the examination certification scheme and managing benefits more generally, go to http://www.apmg-international.com/en/qualifications/managing-benefits/managing-benefits.aspx

Introduction

This guide is about benefits management and is specifically aimed at senior managers – the subject is addressed from a strategic perspective, as much of the detail is included in the companion practitioner guidance, *Managing Benefits* (Jenner, 2014). Many of the technical terms and abbreviations have been removed, although a few remain to ensure that everyone shares a common language (a glossary is also included at the end).

This guide has been written to help you understand what benefits management is and how it addresses the challenges you and your organization face – challenges magnified by tough economic conditions and the need to deliver greater value for money while responding to market and citizen expectations of more customer-focused services. Appropriately designed and applied, benefits management can help address these challenges by optimizing the return on your investments in change.

The guidance is not specific to any one sector: the principles, practices and techniques apply to all sectors of the economy and across jurisdictions.

This guide addresses the following seven key questions in turn:

1. What are benefits and benefits management?
2. Why do you need benefits management and what will you get from it?
3. What are the barriers to success?
4. How do you overcome the barriers to benefits realization?
5. How do you get started and sustain progress?
6. What techniques are available to you?
7. What are the key questions you should be asking?

Before we start, it is worth emphasizing that you are not a passive bystander in this – indeed the extent to which your organization is able to optimize the return on its investments is largely down to the role that you play as a senior manager. You can actively influence the accuracy of benefits forecasting, and the timing and scale of benefits realization. In short, you have the power to make benefits management succeed or fail by ensuring that benefits management practices are combined with effective governance and a value culture.

This guide is designed to provide you with a rapid insight into the practices and techniques used by this emerging discipline. So get involved and positively challenge your project and programme managers, finance and business colleagues – you can make a start by asking them some basic questions, such as those outlined in Chapter 7.

1   What are benefits and benefits management?

Benefits are derived from change initiatives, which include formally constituted projects and programmes. Collectively these initiatives form the organization's change portfolio. Benefits and benefits management are defined as follows:

- **Benefit** The measurable improvement from change, which is perceived as positive by one or more stakeholders, and which contributes to organizational (including strategic) objectives.
- **Benefits management** The identification, quantification, analysis, planning, tracking, realization and optimization of benefits.

The following key points arise from these definitions:

- Benefits are measurable improvements – in terms of, for example, reduced costs, improved customer satisfaction, increased revenue, reduced risk etc.
- Benefits contribute to organizational/strategic objective(s) – consequently:
  - ☐ The logic and assumptions underpinning these objectives need to be clearly articulated so that the contribution benefits make to them can be determined reliably and consistently (techniques such as driver-based analysis can help and are discussed later in this guide).
  - ☐ Benefits from individual initiatives included in the change portfolio should be identified and quantified consistently, and in terms that link to the drivers of the organizational/strategic objectives. So, just as accounting policies are applied to ensure consistency in your organization's accounts, so portfolio-wide benefits eligibility rules should be applied to ensure consistency across the change portfolio. This facilitates level-playing-field investment appraisal and portfolio prioritization;

helps avoid double counting (which distorts the real return on investment); and enables benefits data to be consolidated to provide a portfolio-level picture.

☐ Change initiatives should be designed to realize the benefits that enable achievement of the organization's strategic objectives and business priorities. This is fundamental – benefits should not be used to justify the cost of a change initiative; rather, they represent the rationale for investment. In short, and to borrow from Stephen Covey, we need to 'start with the end in mind' with techniques such as investment/benefits logic mapping.

▪ Benefits are a perceived advantage to stakeholders, including those both within and outside the organization – the latter include customers and shareholders (private sector), citizens, and other departments and agencies (public sector). An active approach to stakeholder engagement is therefore key to effective benefits management.

▪ Benefits management extends from identification of desired benefits through to benefits realization and application of lessons learned. While the practices are broadly sequential, they are characterized by iterative feedback loops, with lessons learned being applied throughout the cycle.

▪ Benefits management is concerned with informing investment decisions and optimization of benefits realization – consequently, it extends beyond passive reporting against forecast benefits to active approaches that engage stakeholders in an ongoing search for emergent or unplanned benefits.

▪ Benefits management seeks to optimize rather than maximize benefits realization. The difference is that, while maximization seeks the most benefits, irrespective of the cost, optimization is about doing the best that can be achieved within constraints (most usually costs but also other constrained resources) and potential alternative uses of the funds available. Thus, realizing 80% of the potential benefits but for only 60% of the cost may be preferred where the savings can be used to fund other initiatives.

Four additional points should also be emphasized:

- There is no one true path to effective benefits management. The practices outlined in this guide should be tailored to the local circumstances, reflecting factors such as your organization's strategic objectives; scale of investment in change initiatives; the complexity of those initiatives; existing strategic planning, project and programme, financial, performance and risk management processes; experience and track record in terms of benefits realization; governance structure; and culture. The companion practitioner guide includes examples of how organizations have adapted these practices in a variety of situations, as well as guidance on when the relevant techniques are appropriate.
- While the practice of benefits management needs to be tailored to the specific organizational circumstances, someone needs to own the key responsibilities identified, and in particular:
  - ☐ Responsibility should be clearly allocated for delivering each of the enabling products/services and business changes upon which benefits realization is dependent.
  - ☐ Benefit owners must be identified for each significant benefit.
  - ☐ Someone should have overall accountability for benefits realization from each change initiative – typically the senior responsible owner (SRO).
- It is crucial that we avoid creating a parallel industry that treats benefits management as a separate discipline. This is costly and ineffective. Benefits management should be coordinated with, and wherever possible integrated into, the wider organizational context – and in particular the organization's strategic planning, project and programme,

financial and performance management systems. This is illustrated in Figure 1.1.

- What arises from this is that:
  - ☐ While there is a place for benefits management specialists, such specialists should clearly support and mentor business managers in the delivery of benefits-led change initiatives.
  - ☐ Benefits management is not an additional bureaucracy or new 'cottage industry'. Yes, benefits management comes with a price tag and needs to be appropriately resourced, but it's one that should be more than paid for by the improvements in benefits actually realized. Indeed, applied with intelligence, effective benefits management may be achieved with less effort than is currently expended – as long as: change initiatives are set up to succeed from the start; we focus on the key benefits; and we integrate the approach more effectively with the functions and activities identified in Figure 1.1.

While the focus in investment decision-making should be on realism, the approach to benefits realization should be characterized by enthusiasm, to help overcome the obstacles that can often arise during initiative delivery. Your role is crucial in this regard – in championing the implementation and application of benefits management and by maintaining a focus on the sources of competitive advantage outlined in the next chapter.

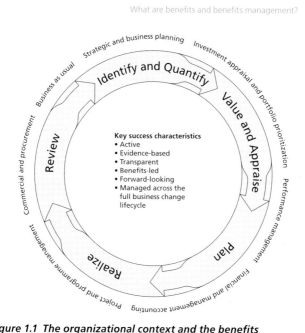

Figure 1.1 The organizational context and the benefits management cycle

2 Why do you need benefits management and what will you get from it?

As stated earlier, the rationale for investments in change (whether these initiatives are established informally or formally as projects or programmes) is the realization of benefits. Unfortunately, the evidence paints a disappointing picture as far as benefits realization is concerned – for example, the UK National Audit Office (NAO, 2011) reports that 'the evidence shows that two-thirds of public sector projects are completed late, over budget or do not deliver the outcomes expected' and 'The track record of project delivery in the private sector is equally mixed.'

The problem appears to cross all project types – in the United States, Lovallo and Kahneman (2003) note that 'Most large capital investments come in late and over budget, never living up to expectations. More than 70% of new manufacturing plants in North America, for example, close within their first decade of operation. Approximately three-quarters of mergers and acquisitions never pay off … And efforts to enter new markets fare no better; the vast majority end up being abandoned within a few years.'

Similarly, change management 'guru' John Kotter (APM, 2009) says, 'Up to 70% of change initiatives fail to deliver on the benefits that they set out to achieve.'

And things don't appear to be improving – a report from Moorhouse Consulting (2009a) for the *Financial Times* found that 'we still see most organisations struggling to deliver sustainable benefits from their change programmes. There is also scant evidence of any maturation in the discipline of benefits realisation generally.'

But where progress can be made, the benefits are significant – a study by Ward *et al.* (2008) found that while the adoption of more structured approaches to initiative delivery had not resulted in increased benefits realization, the adoption of key benefits management-related practices was associated with increased benefits realization.

So, the fundamental driver for benefits management is the consistently reported poor track record of change initiatives in realizing the benefits they were established to deliver. The corollary is that where you are able to address this, significant competitive advantage can accrue to your organization from:

- More reliable information on which to make investment decisions – as forecast benefits are more accurate, complete, and are clearly linked to the organization's strategic objectives and business priorities.
- Increased realization of forecast benefits by ensuring the required enabling, business and behavioural change takes place – so that performance of the investment matches the 'promise'.
- Benefits are realized as early as possible and are sustained for as long as possible.
- Emergent benefits are captured and leveraged (and any dis-benefits are minimized) – so optimizing the benefits realized and value for money achieved.
- More efficient use of available resources – delivering more from less.
- Enhanced ability to attract and retain motivated and skilled change management staff.
- The ability to demonstrate all of the above:
  - As part of the framework of accountability, so that the confidence of investors and funding agencies is maintained, thereby safeguarding future investments.
  - As a basis for continuous improvement from learning about what works.

3 What are the barriers to success?

The benefits of benefits management outlined in the previous chapter are not automatic – a survey by the Association for Project Management (APM) and Chartered Institute of Management Accountants (CIMA) in Ireland in 2012 found that less than half of respondents described their organization's approach as 'formal/structured' and only 3% indicated that it provided value all of the time. Addressing this calls for effective implementation and operation of benefits management approaches that overcome the following four barriers.

3.1 BARRIER 1: COMMON MISCONCEPTIONS ABOUT BENEFITS REALIZATION

There are a number of misconceptions that compromise the effectiveness of benefits management and the realization of benefits in practice. These include the incorrect assumption that benefits just happen: i.e. all we need to do is to complete the initiative and the benefits that were included in the business case will automatically be realized. This misconception manifests itself in the confusion of business and enabling changes (a new IT system and training programme, for example) and the benefits that arise from those changes (realization of time savings that can be re-allocated to realize productivity improvements etc.). This misconception also results in an underestimation of the focus required to realize the benefits. For example, research undertaken by Donald Marchand (2004) at IMD shows that IT can deliver business value, but the key is usage, not deployment. Marchand argues that while organizations devote 90% of their efforts to deployment, this only accounts for 25% of the business value. In contrast, relatively little effort is directed at realizing the 75% of value that derives from increased usage of information. In practice, realization of the potential benefits is often dependent on business change or some other dedicated management effort, such as redeploying staff or the time saved from redesigning processes.

3.2   BARRIER 2: THE KNOWING–DOING GAP

Pfeffer and Sutton (2000) argue that there is a paradox in many areas of management, in that good practice is known but rarely applied. There is evidence that this applies to benefits management where much of the guidance has been around for a decade, and yet many organizations struggle to implement it effectively. Reasons for this include: the common misconceptions referred to in the previous paragraph; talk is a lot easier than action; absence of defined responsibilities; the tendency to fall back on old habits; not taking benefits seriously enough; and the multi-disciplinary and cross-functional nature of benefits management.

3.3   BARRIER 3: COGNITIVE BIAS

In many cases the causes of failure can be traced back to the business case. Why might this be?

Psychologists have identified a series of cognitive biases that adversely affect the production of accurate benefits forecasts – for example, Lovallo and Kahneman (2003) argue in the *Harvard Business Review* that forecasters suffer from 'delusional optimism: we overemphasise projects' potential benefits and underestimate likely costs, spinning success scenarios while ignoring the possibility of mistakes.' Table 3.1 identifies five of the main cognitive biases and the impact they have on benefits forecasting.

The most powerful of these cognitive biases is simple overconfidence, or what is termed optimism bias. What makes such biases so powerful is that even when we are aware of them, we can fall foul of them. Research by Moorhouse Consulting (2009b) has found that 'only 10% of SROs feel business cases and benefits realisation are adequately understood on programmes across government and industry; however over 60% feel the understanding on their own programmes is adequate' – an example of the planning fallacy in action.

Table 3.1 Cognitive biases affecting benefits forecasting

Cognitive bias	Impact on benefits forecasting
Expectation or confirmation bias	The tendency for forecasters to select evidence that confirms existing beliefs and assumptions, and discount or ignore evidence that conflicts with these beliefs.
The planning fallacy	The belief that, while being aware that many similar initiatives have failed to realize the forecast benefits in the past, this won't affect the current initiative.
The framing effect and loss aversion	The tendency to value losses avoided more than equivalent gains. Hastie and Dawes (2001) note that 'most empirical estimates conclude that losses are about twice as painful as gains are pleasurable'. Thus business cases that are framed in terms of what might go wrong if the initiative were not to proceed appear more compelling than if the same initiative's business case is prepared on the basis of the positive outcomes obtained.

Cognitive bias	Impact on benefits forecasting
Anchoring and adjustment	In preparing forecasts we 'anchor' on, and give disproportionate weight to, the first estimate (no matter how reliable or relevant) and then make insufficient adjustment to reflect the specific circumstances. A provision of 10% contingency is therefore rarely sufficient.
Groupthink	The tendency to confuse knowledge with assumptions – and this tendency is reinforced when the majority of those involved share the same set of beliefs and values. Thus we become overly confident in our forecasts and ignore counter-information.

But another explanation for forecasting errors has also been proposed – and it is one where the cause lies less in the cognitive biases that affect us as individuals, and more in organizational factors.

3.4 BARRIER 4: ORGANIZATIONAL PRESSURES

Bent Flyvbjerg at Oxford University has undertaken extensive research on transportation infrastructure projects – research with a global reach. He concludes that forecasts are 'highly, systematically and significantly misleading (inflated). The result is large benefit shortfalls.' The cause is what he terms as 'strategic misrepresentation', which is defined as 'the planned, systematic, deliberate misstatement of costs and benefits to get projects approved'. In short, 'that is lying' (Flyvbjerg *et al.*, 2005).

This is not restricted to transportation initiatives – comparative research finds the same issues apply to a wide range of projects: concert halls, museums, sports arenas, convention centres, urban renewal schemes, power plants, dams, IT systems, oil and gas exploration, aerospace projects, new product development etc. (Flyvbjerg, 2006).

Other academics have reached similar conclusions – for example, in Australia, Lin *et al*. (2005) report that 26.2% of respondents to their survey admitted to regularly overstating benefits in order to get their business cases approved. Ward reports an even more depressing situation in Europe, with 38% of respondents in one survey undertaken by Cranfield University openly admitting to overstating benefits to get funding (Ward, 2006) – with the traditional investment appraisal process being 'seen as a ritual that must be overcome before any project can begin' (Peppard *et al*., 2007).

The cause is, according to Professor Flyvbjerg, either because it's in the economic interests of those making the case, or because it is expected by the project sponsor in support of 'pet' projects. In short, benefits are used to help justify the investment in a preferred solution – so the emphasis is on identifying benefits, not as a basis for managing their realization, but in order to justify the costs required. The result is that those benefits are overstated and there is little focus on realizing them in practice.

Solutions to these barriers are discussed in the next chapter.

4 How do you overcome the barriers to benefits realization?

Successfully addressing the barriers outlined in the last chapter requires that our approach to benefits management should recognize six key success characteristics. In other words, benefits management should be:

- **Active** Rather than passive tracking against forecast benefits, the focus is on an active search for benefits, via ongoing participative stakeholder engagement.
- **Evidence-based** Forecasts and practices are driven by evidence about what works rather than assumptions and advocacy.
- **Transparent** Activities are based on open and honest forecasting and reporting, with a 'clear line of sight' from strategic objectives to benefits forecast and realized.
- **Benefits-led** Just as we expect change initiatives and the portfolio to be benefits-led, so too should benefits management be focused on the difference it is making.
- **Forward-looking** The emphasis is on learning and continuous improvement, rather than the backward-looking attribution of blame.
- **Managed across the full business change lifecycle** Benefits management extends from benefits identification through to realization and applying lessons learned. But to emphasize – it is not a linear, bureaucratic process concerned with passive monitoring against forecast. Rather it is crucial that iterative feedback loops are applied all the way through the benefits management cycle, with lessons being actively sought and applied throughout as a basis for learning and continuous improvement.

All these key success characteristics require senior managers who actively exhibit and promote such behaviour. Beyond these characteristics, effective benefits management is dependent on the seven principles and disciplined application of the practices shown in the benefits management model at Figure 4.1. (Note that the principles and practices reflect insights and lessons learned from a variety of disciplines – not only project and programme management (PPM) but also management accounting, economics, behavioural finance, change management, systems thinking, psychology and neuroscience.)

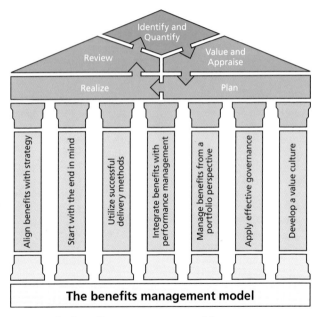

Figure 4.1 The benefits management model

4.1 BENEFITS MANAGEMENT PRINCIPLES

The seven principles represent the foundations upon which successful benefits management practices are built. These principles are:

1. **Align benefits with strategy** Benefits represent measurable improvements which contribute towards one or more organizational or strategic objectives. It is therefore crucial that strategy is clearly articulated so that this contribution can be assessed reliably and consistently. Techniques include examples of driver-based analysis such as the service profit chain (see Figure 4.2) and service value chain, where the drivers of the key elements in the organization's business model are clearly defined.

2. **Start with the end in mind** Schaffer and Thomson (1992) argue that one cause of business change failure is that organizations 'confuse ends with means, processes with outcomes' and pursue 'activities that sound good, look good, and allow managers to feel good – but in fact contribute little or nothing to bottom-line performance'. Organizations consequently too often make the mistake of investing in activity-centred change initiatives without sufficient focus on the ultimate benefits because of a mistaken assumption that improved performance will just happen. The problems are that the linkages between such

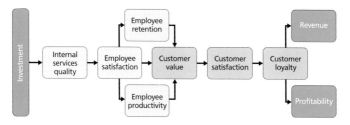

Figure 4.2 The service profit chain

activities and the organization's objectives are not made clear (hence the need for the driver-based analysis mentioned previously), and often several of these initiatives are launched in an uncoordinated manner with all of them claiming to deliver the same benefits. The result is 'wave after wave of programs rolled across the landscape with little positive impact' (Beer *et al.*, 1990). The solution lies with benefits-led change, where initiatives are established to realize the required benefits, rather than benefits being used to justify a pre-selected solution. A technique that can help is investment logic mapping, as developed in Victoria, Australia. Here, before a business case is prepared, workshops are held that focus on defining the problem, identifying the benefits sought and outlining the required solution for delivering them.

3. **Utilize successful delivery methods** By combining appropriately tailored delivery methods with effective approaches to change management, benefits realization is enabled. But in a world characterized by complexity, ambiguity and uncertainty, we also need to give greater emphasis to:

- Rigorous start gates
- Modular, agile and incremental development approaches, breaking large initiatives down into smaller ones of shorter duration
- Incremental rather than one-off investment decisions, based on the technique of 'staged release of funding' with continued release of funding being linked more closely to confidence in benefits realization
- A forward-looking perspective, where the focus is less on strictly holding people to account for forecast benefits than on a continuous search for insights and emergent benefits.

4. **Integrate benefits with performance management**
Wherever possible, benefits (and the measures used) should be integrated into the organization's operational and HR performance management systems. Such integration should include:

- For operational performance management:
    - Linking benefits to the organization's key performance indicators: for example, via the balanced scorecard (Kaplan and Norton, 1996) where benefits are expressed in terms of their impact on the measures established in each perspective – financial, customer, internal business process, and learning and growth.
    - Building benefits into business plans and budgets via the technique of 'booking the benefits' – i.e. reflecting the forecast benefits in organizational targets.
- For HR performance management:
    - Aligning responsibilities for benefits management with individuals' performance objectives – so that there is clarity about what people are responsible and accountable for, including implementing the changes upon which benefits realization depends.
    - Aligning responsibilities for benefits management with the reward and recognition processes – via 'booking the benefits' in individual performance targets.

5. **Manage benefits from a portfolio perspective** Consistent approaches should be applied to all initiatives within the change portfolio, including:

- The classification and valuation of benefits in business cases
- Benefits-led investment appraisal and portfolio prioritization
- Effective management of dependencies between change initiatives
- Tracking benefits realization beyond initiative closure.

The benefits of a portfolio approach include the following:

- It helps minimize double counting
- It ensures that good practice is repeatable
- Lessons learned are applied widely
- A focus on benefits realization extends beyond initiative closure
- The organization can come to an informed view as to whether the benefits realized represent the best possible return on its accumulated investment in change – via a regularly updated portfolio-level benefits realization plan and benefits dashboard report.

6. **Apply effective governance** This includes ensuring that there is clear accountability and responsibility for the enabling and business changes upon which benefits realization is dependent, and for realization of the required benefits.

7. **Develop a value culture** Such a culture takes benefits and benefits management seriously, and focuses on creating and sustaining value from an organization's investments in change. This is aided by focusing on three interrelated factors (Beer *et al.*, 1990):

- Coordination – ensuring that sufficient attention is given to opportunities for sharing and disseminating lessons learned across the organization. A benefits management forum can be useful here.
- Commitment – to drive 'the effort, initiative and cooperation that coordinated action demands.' As was said earlier about the key success characteristics of effective benefits management, your personal and visible commitment as a senior manager is crucial.
- Competencies – ensuring sufficient and ongoing training to build and enhance the competencies and capabilities within the organization.

4.2   BENEFITS MANAGEMENT PRACTICES

The benefits management cycle shown in Figure 1.1 consists of five practices. While these practices are broadly sequential, they are also characterized by iterative feedback loops, with insights being applied throughout the cycle. The five practices are as follows:

1. **Identify and Quantify** This practice lays the basis for: informed options analysis, investment appraisal, and portfolio prioritization; and the management of benefits realization in due course. The Identify and Quantify practice achieves this by:

   ■ Identification of benefits via benefits discovery workshops, benefits mapping and customer/user insight techniques
   ■ Quantification of benefits – overcoming the cognitive biases and strategic misrepresentation discussed in Chapter 3 by, for example, reference class and probability-based forecasting (see Chapter 6).

   Your role as a senior manager includes: encouraging accurate and reliable forecasts (including asking forecasters what their track record is like in producing accurate forecasts); asking whether all potential benefits have been identified from each initiative; and – crucially – ensuring that initiatives are set up to succeed by starting with the end in mind (see section 4.1, point 2).

2. **Value and Appraise** Here the objective is to ensure that resources are allocated to those change initiatives which individually and collectively represent the best value for money. The Value and Appraise practice achieves this by:

   ■ Valuing financial and non-financial benefits in monetary terms to facilitate options analysis, investment appraisal and portfolio prioritization. Non-financial benefits can be valued in monetary terms using econometric techniques such as willingness to pay or accept.

■ Appraisal of options and initiatives via four methods of investment appraisal. These are: cost-benefit analysis; real options analysis; cost-effectiveness analysis; and multi-criteria analysis. It is important to apply the appropriate technique to the circumstances: where initiatives are designed to increase revenue or reduce cost, cost-benefit analysis is most appropriate; where there is a high degree of uncertainty, real options analysis can be of value; where initiatives are mandatory, cost-effectiveness analysis is relevant; and where the investment objective involves achieving some defined strategic contribution, multi-criteria analysis is often most appropriate.

Your role as a senior manager includes ensuring that all feasible options are identified; that the benefits used in investment appraisals and for portfolio prioritization are robust and realizable (by applying a portfolio-wide set of benefits eligibility rules); and that the investment appraisal technique applied is relevant to the type of initiative.

3. **Plan** The Plan practice ensures accountability and transparency for: the realization of identified benefits; the changes on which they are dependent; the mitigation of dis-benefits; and the identification and leveraging of emergent benefits. This is achieved via the following key elements:

■ Validating the benefits forecast by agreeing them with the recipients
■ Prioritizing benefits
■ Managing pre-transition activity
■ Selecting appropriate benefit measures
■ Managing benefits threats and opportunities (ensuring emergent benefits are fully exploited)
■ Planning effective stakeholder engagement and communications

■ Preparing benefits documentation, including a benefits realization plan and dashboard report at both initiative and portfolio levels.

Your role as a senior manager includes ensuring that the foundations for success are laid by ensuring that responsibility for benefits realization is clearly defined; looking beyond the forecast to arrangements for exploiting emergent benefits; and, fundamentally, asking whether, at a portfolio level, the planned benefits represent the best that can be achieved from the organization's accumulated investment in change.

4. **Realize** The objective of this practice is to optimize benefits realization by actively managing planned benefits through to their realization; capturing and leveraging emergent benefits; and mitigating any dis-benefits. This includes ensuring that the business and behavioural changes on which benefits realization is dependent actually take place. The Realize practice achieves this by the following key elements:

■ **Transition management** Ensuring that initiative outputs are fit for purpose and can be integrated into business operations.

■ **Tracking and reporting benefits realization** And taking appropriate action where required. Effective management of benefits realization is aided by the selection of a suite of measures, including leading and lagging measures, proxy indicators, evidence events, case studies, surveys and stories. In this way we can create a 'rich picture' providing feedback on benefits realization from multiple perspectives. Effective management of benefits realization is also aided by techniques including 'one version of the truth', 'management by exception' and 'clear line of sight reporting' (see Chapter 6).

■ **Winning hearts and minds** Going beyond processes and practices to consider the softer side of business change, and in particular the people dimension (behavioural change). This can be enabled by a range of strategies including:

- ☐ Aligning personal incentives with benefits realization
- ☐ Adopting new routines
- ☐ Applying insights from the fields of behavioural finance, psychology and neuroscience
- ☐ Developing measures that engage users in terms that make sense to them
- ☐ Utilizing 'narrative leadership'. Your role here as a senior manager is crucial, for as Dearing *et al.* (2002) say, 'We shy away from forceful demands for loyalty and commitment, but we flock to and swarm round focal points where 'cool stuff' seems either to be happening or about to happen. Good leaders work with our hunger to involve ourselves, with others, in interesting work and exciting projects.' Guidance on how this can be achieved, along with real-life examples, is contained within the companion practitioner guide.

Your role as a senior manager includes ensuring that benefits realization is monitored on an active basis with prompt corrective action being taken to:

- ◼ Address emerging shortfalls on planned benefits
- ◼ Mitigate dis-benefits
- ◼ Identify and leverage emergent benefits.

5. **Review** The objectives of the Review practice are to ensure and assure that:

- ◼ Forecast benefits are achievable and continue to represent value for money
- ◼ Appropriate arrangements have been made for benefits monitoring, management and evaluation
- ◼ Benefits realization is being effectively managed
- ◼ Lessons are learned for both the current initiative and as a basis for more effective benefits management practices across the change portfolio.

This practice encompasses independent reviews as well as those undertaken on behalf of the senior responsible owner (SRO)/project executive:

- At the commencement of an initiative – start gates (independent) and pre-mortems (for the SRO/project executive).
- During the lifetime of an initiative – 'in-flight' reviews, including those undertaken at the end of a tranche within a programme (for the SRO/project executive) and those at mandated stage/phase gates (independent).
- After implementation – post-implementation (for the SRO/project executive) and post-investment reviews (independent).

Your role as a senior manager includes ensuring that regular reviews occur throughout the business change lifecycle; that effective checks are undertaken to compare benefits realized with those forecast; and that lessons learned are identified and applied.

5   How do you get started and sustain progress?

5.1   GETTING STARTED

The approach to implementation will vary according to the circumstances, including the scale of senior management support and whether the organization is operating in a stable or dynamic environment. That said, experience indicates that early consideration should be given to the following 10 key steps:

1. Ensure that the value chain underpinning the strategic objectives or the organization's business model is made explicit by asking the following questions: What are the elements in the value chain? What factors drive achievement of each element? How are these elements linked? This will enable consistent appraisal of the strategic contribution of each change initiative. Techniques that assist here include the service profit chain (see Figure 4.2), the service value chain and the balanced scorecard.

2. Set up initiatives to succeed by 'starting with the end in mind' – ensuring clarity about the problem to be solved or the opportunity to be exploited. Only then should work begin on scoping the required solution and developing the business case.

3. Compile a portfolio benefits management framework, including benefits eligibility rules, so that benefits are expressed consistently. This helps to prevent double counting, lays the basis for more effective investment appraisal and portfolio prioritization, and facilitates consolidation of a portfolio-level view on benefits realization.

4. Implement consistent approaches to benefits mapping to identify the enabling and business changes upon which benefits realization is dependent and to link benefits to the strategic objectives.

5. Adopt the technique of 'staged release of funding', where continued funding for initiatives is dependent upon incremental benefits exceeding the costs required to realize them, and continuing stakeholder commitment to the realization of those benefits.

6. Ensure clarity about the key benefits on the major initiatives in your organization's change portfolio. Starting with the top five benefits from each initiative, find out what they are, how they will be measured, who's responsible for ensuring they are realized and when they will be realized.

7. Consolidate the information collected above into a portfolio benefits realization plan so that it is clear what benefits will be realized in the forthcoming period. This then enables the following questions to be answered: Is this scale of benefits sufficient given the investment made? Can anything be done to improve the position?

8. Track and report progress against the portfolio benefits realization plan on a regular basis (at least quarterly) to ensure that performance matches the promise – and apply the techniques of:

    ■ Management by exception – to focus attention on the most material variances from plan
    ■ One version of the truth – to ensure reliability of management information on benefits realized.

9. Implement post-implementation review on all change initiatives, with independent post-investment review for those initiatives that warrant it. This provides a basis for identifying improvements to the benefits management practices and the collection of a reference class of benefits data to inform future forecasting.

10. Organize a series of briefing sessions to raise awareness of the importance of benefits management, explaining what is required and what forms of assistance will be available. This should encompass all stakeholders, but with a particular focus on senior management. Techniques that can facilitate senior management engagement include:

   ■ Journey mapping – where activities and events are mapped to a schedule so that senior managers are clear about what will be seen, by when and what difference it will make.
   ■ Decision-conferencing – where senior managers openly debate the merits of individual initiatives (including their benefits and strategic contribution) and the portfolio as a whole.

5.2   HOW DO WE SUSTAIN PROGRESS?

Practical experience indicates that implementation is often less of an issue than sustaining progress – and establishing a value culture where benefits management is business as usual is rarely quick or easy. The lessons learned from those that have overcome these obstacles are that continued progress is facilitated by the following six factors:

1. Effective governance, including:

   ■ Having a board-level sponsor, or champion, to maintain focus at the highest level, and to continually promote benefits management across the organization
   ■ Creating 'apostles' for the approach across the organization and bringing them together in a benefits management forum to share experiences, insights and lessons learned
   ■ Building cross-board commitment – influential non-executive directors can play an important role in this regard.

2. Treating the development of benefits management as a (benefits-led) business and behavioural change programme. This includes:

    ■ Aligning the reward and recognition processes with appropriate behaviours – and applying them through objective-setting and personal reviews. This is especially important for senior management, programme managers and budget holders.

    ■ Recognizing that behavioural change can follow the adoption of new roles and practices – so, for example, ensuring that benefits management is a regular item on the board agenda and applying the technique of decision-conferencing (as referred to above)

    ■ Adopting a benefits-led rather than activity-centred approach. This means that the focus should be less on what benefits management processes to introduce, and more on the improvements required, which therefore drives the selection of appropriate solutions.

3. Ongoing stakeholder engagement in the development of benefits management. This is achieved by:

    ■ Application of the champion-challenger model whereby processes are open to challenge and improvement, but until successfully challenged, all participants agree to adhere to the current process. This helps to ensure that stakeholders are actively involved in the development of benefits management practices rather than perceiving them as something that is imposed on them.

    ■ Focusing on the following four core stakeholder groups: senior management (including the board); operational managers responsible for benefits realization; project and programme managers responsible for delivery; and those responsible for business change (APM, 2011).

- Documenting the agreed processes in a portfolio benefits management framework which is accessible (e.g. via the intranet) and under change control. It's important that people know what is expected of them.
- Demonstrating the benefits of benefits management with some quick wins.
- Delivering a programme of ongoing benefits management workshops, seminars and master classes – supported by ongoing coaching and mentoring.

4. Measuring progress, encompassing both:

 - Practice maturity – using the health-check assessment in Chapter 7
 - Impact – to assess whether the benefits outlined in Chapter 2 are being realized.

5. Appropriate use of software – software solutions can help to embed benefits management and save time and resources (but the adoption of effective practices and governance comes first).

6. Relevant training and development – to build the skills and competencies of staff with a role in the successful delivery of change. It is also important that the organization's management development programmes encompass realizing benefits from change initiatives. Benefits specialists can play a crucial role in coaching and mentoring staff with an emphasis on increasing their skills to take on the role as part of business as usual. Indeed, research finds that while productivity improves following training, with follow-up coaching the improvement can be three times as great.

6 What techniques are available to you?

Managing Benefits (Jenner, 2014) identifies a range of techniques that address the issues which adversely impact the effectiveness of benefits management in practice. Some of the main techniques are outlined in this guide and are summarized in Table 6.1.

Table 6.1 Key benefits management techniques

Problem/issue	Relevant technique
Unreliable forecasts in business cases undermine the investment appraisal and portfolio prioritization processes	**Reference class forecasting** A technique where forecasts of an initiative's duration, costs and benefits are derived from what actually occurred in a reference class of similar initiatives. **Delphi technique** A technique where forecasts are derived from a panel of subject-matter experts who provide their estimates anonymously and then revise them in the light of the estimates of their peers. But in order to guard against 'Groupthink', it is crucial that: ■ The group making the forecasts is diverse and independent – as Surowiecki (2004) says, 'The best collective decisions are the product of disagreement and contest, not consensus and compromise.'

Table continues

Table 6.1 continued

Problem/issue	Relevant technique
	■ The group should make its forecasts anonymously – as Solomon Asch demonstrated in a classic psychology experiment, there is a strong pull towards conformity and this can influence people's judgements. So ensure the initial forecasts are made without knowledge of what others are estimating.
	Probability-based forecasting
	Rather than using single-point forecasts, probabilities can be assigned to a range of outcomes, or can be calculated using a 'Monte Carlo' simulation. Alternatively, we can avoid the issues around assessing probabilities, while still recognizing the uncertainty inherent in forecasting, by estimating using optimistic, pessimistic and most likely scenarios.
Strategic objectives are set at such a high level that reliably determining the contribution of individual initiatives, and the portfolio as a whole, is difficult	**Driver-based analysis**
	A technique whereby the implicit value chain underpinning the strategic objectives, or the organization's business model, is made explicit – i.e. what are the elements in the value chain, what factors drive achievement of each element, and how are they linked? This can be achieved using approaches such as the service profit chain, the service value chain and the balanced scorecard.

Problem/issue	Relevant technique
Initiatives are started without a clear idea of the benefits that will be realized	**Investment logic mapping** The story of an investment on a single page in a form that can be easily understood and adapted to represent a changing story. It shows: ■ The drivers or the problem at hand, along with the high-level strategic interventions proposed to address the problem ■ The benefits to the organization and its customers that result from addressing the problem (these will be supported by at least one or two key performance indicators, with associated targets for each benefit, which are meaningful, attributable and measurable) ■ The business changes and enabling assets required to realize those benefits.
It is not clear how the initiative will lead to benefits realization or how these benefits will contribute to the strategic objectives	**Benefits map** A pictorial representation of the business and enabling changes on which benefits realization depends, showing how these benefits contribute to organizational (including strategic) objectives.

Table continues

Table 6.1 continued

Problem/issue	Relevant technique
Benefits are stated in different terms in each business case, making comparing initiatives and consolidating data problematic	**Benefits eligibility rules** The set of rules applying to all initiatives, covering what benefits can and can't be claimed, how they should be categorized, quantified and valued.
Initiatives are started without a real understanding of customers' needs	**Customer insight** Defined by the Government Communication Network's Engage Programme as: 'A deep "truth" about the customer, based on their behaviour, experiences, beliefs, needs or desires, that is relevant to the task or issue and "rings bells" with target people.'
Cost-benefit appraisals do not adequately take into account non-financial and qualitative factors	**Multi-criteria analysis** Consideration of benefits under two main headings: ■ Return or attractiveness – including financial return and strategic contribution ■ Risk or achievability – including likelihood of benefits realization.

Problem/issue	Relevant technique
Potential benefits are not always identified and initiatives stop searching for additional benefits once they meet the organization's hurdle rate of return	**The 'dog that didn't bark' test** Assessing not only the identified benefits, but also asking whether there are any additional benefits that haven't been included (name of test comes from the Sherlock Holmes' story *Silver Blaze*). This is referred to by Kahneman (2011) as 'WYSIATI' ('What You See Is All There Is'). The risk is that we only consider the benefits included in the business case rather than asking what other benefits may be possible.
We struggle to maintain focus on benefits after the initiative has been approved	**Booking the benefits** Whereby forecast benefits are 'booked' in budgets, headcount targets, unit costs and organization and individual performance targets.
Lack of active participation by senior management in the benefits management cycle	**Decision-conferencing** A technique whereby managers consider and debate in a facilitated workshop the relative weightings to attach to the organization's strategic objectives; the criteria to be used to assess the strategic contribution in each case; and the scores to allocate to individual initiatives. In this way the portfolio governance body comes to a collective decision on the composition of the portfolio. This has been found to be very effective in terms of optimizing portfolio returns and also results in enhanced commitment to the change portfolio and to the realization of benefits.

Table continues

Table 6.1 continued

Problem/issue	Relevant technique
Lack of clarity about what change initiatives are under way, the forecast benefits and the anticipated contribution to strategic objectives	**'Clear line of sight' planning and reporting** A technique that ensures a transparent view from strategic intent through to benefits realization. This is aided by the preparation of: ■ A portfolio-level benefits realization plan showing what benefits will be realized in the forthcoming period from the organization's accumulated investment in change ■ A portfolio-level benefits dashboard report showing progress against the benefits realization plan.
Confusion as to when management action needs to be considered in response to benefits realization varying from plan	**Management by exception** A technique by which variances from plan that exceed a pre-set control limit (e.g. by +/−10%) are escalated for management attention.

Problem/issue	Relevant technique
Confusion as to the current state of progress on individual initiatives within the change portfolio	**One version of the truth** A technique whereby each element of progress reporting by change initiatives (including benefits) is derived from an agreed source and to an agreed schedule. The resulting data is recognized as the authoritative source of information on portfolio and initiative progress used for monitoring, reporting and management decision-making.
Unplanned or emergent benefits are not always identified and fully exploited	**'Scout and beacon' approach** As advocated by Andrew and Sirkin (2006), where capturing emergent benefits is aided by: ■ 'Scouts' who scan the environment for potential opportunities ■ 'Beacons' which are 'lit', clearly communicating that information on emergent benefits is welcomed.
Funding allocations are not amended to reflect shifts in strategic objectives and business priorities	**Staged release of funding** Funding is released to initiatives as they pass through the various stage/phase gates as part of the business change lifecycle – with funding being limited to that required to take the initiative through to the next stage/phase gate review. In this way, the organization's commitment of resources is linked to assessment of performance, continued strategic alignment and confidence in benefits realization.

Table continues

Table 6.1 continued

Problem/issue	Relevant technique
Lack of active engagement by stakeholders in the benefits management practices	**Champion-challenger model** A technique where all change initiatives are expected to comply with the defined portfolio processes and regulations (the current 'champion') but everyone is encouraged to recommend changes ('challengers'). When approved, the 'challenger' becomes the new 'champion' process.

7 What are the key questions you should be asking?

We finish with the health-check assessment from the practitioner guide. We encourage you to assess your change portfolio using these 10 simple questions. Suggested actions to address specific weaknesses are included in *Managing Benefits* (Jenner, 2014). Repeating the assessment on a periodic basis (and by comparing the assessments made with those of your peers and other stakeholders) can be used to assess the extent to which the organization is making progress in optimizing the return from its investments in change.

Table 7.1 Health-check assessment

Key benefits management statements	Always	Usually	Occasion-ally	Never
1. The benefits from our change initiative(s) are clearly identified in measurable terms that demonstrate strategic contribution.				
2. Benefits forecasts are robust and realizable.				

Table continues

Table 7.1 continued

Key benefits management statements	Always	Usually	Occasion-ally	Never
3. Benefits are expressed and quantified consistently by all change initiatives, so enabling reliable portfolio prioritization.				
4. Responsibilities are clearly defined for realizing each benefit and for delivering the business and enabling changes on which benefits realization is dependent.				
5. We don't stop at the hurdle rate of return, but instead look for all potential benefits.				

Key benefits management statements	Always	Usually	Occasion-ally	Never
6. The investment rationale and value-for-money position is tested on a regular basis with formal recommitment to benefits realization so that there are no 'orphan' initiatives.				
7. Measures used provide a 'rich picture' on benefits realization, and rather than encouraging perverse incentives, they engage the user in exceeding those forecast.				

Table continues

Table 7.1 continued

Key benefits management statements	Always	Usually	Occasion-ally	Never
8. Benefits realization is monitored on an active basis with prompt corrective action being taken to address emerging shortfalls and to mitigate known and emergent dis-benefits.				
9. Effective action is taken to identify and leverage emergent benefits.				
10. Checks are undertaken to assess whether the performance matched the promise and identify and apply lessons learned.				

It is also helpful to learn from others – issues are rarely unique and someone somewhere has probably had to grapple with the issues you are facing today. The companion practitioner guidance provides a source of helpful information on various approaches to common issues.

There is also a dedicated community of interest at:

http://www.linkedin.com/groups/Managing-Benefits-4493501

where you can post questions and requests for advice.

For further information about the examination certification scheme and managing benefits more generally, see:

http://www.apmg-international.com/en/qualifications/managing-benefits/managing-benefits.aspx

Glossary

APMG International
The accreditation body and examination institute for all 'Best Management Practice' and other related qualifications.

behavioural economics/finance
The study of the effects of psychology on investment decision-making and financial management.

benefit owner
The individual responsible for the realization of a benefit and who agrees the benefit profile prepared by the business change manager.

benefits eligibility rules
The set of rules about what benefits can and can't be claimed, how they should be categorized, quantified and valued.

benefits management
The identification, quantification, analysis, planning, tracking, realization and optimization of benefits.

benefits management forum
A group of practitioners from all relevant disciplines. Established to share and disseminate lessons learned across the organization.

benefits realization plan
The plan that provides a consolidated view of the benefits forecast by type/category and which represents the baseline against which benefits realization can be monitored and evaluated.

business as usual (BAU)
The routine, day-to-day operational activities by which an organization pursues its mission.

business model
A cause-and-effect model which describes the assumptions about how the organization creates and delivers value to customers or citizens.

cost-benefit analysis
Analysis which quantifies in monetary terms as many of the costs and benefits of a proposal as feasible, including items for which the market does not provide a satisfactory measure of economic value (HM Treasury, 2003).

cost-effectiveness analysis
Analysis that compares the cost of alternative ways of producing the same or similar outputs (HM Treasury, 2003).

dis-benefit
The measurable result of a change, perceived as negative by one or more stakeholders, which detracts from one or more organizational (including strategic) objectives.

emergent benefits
Benefits that emerge during the design, development, deployment and application of the new ways of working, rather than being identified at the start of the initiative.

evidence events
Events that can be observed and which provide evidence that the benefit has been realized. These can be stated in the form of a 'date with destiny'; for example, 'Three months from today, the SRO will visit a front-line office and discuss the improvements seen with staff and customers'.

governance
The set of policies, regulations, functions, processes, procedures and responsibilities that define the establishment, management and control of projects, programmes or portfolios (APM, 2013).

Groupthink

A term used to describe a group's style of thinking where the maintenance of the group's cohesion and togetherness becomes more important than the actual decision. Janis (1972) defined it as 'a way of deliberating that group members use when their desire for unanimity overrides their motivation to assess all available plans of action'.

hurdle rate of return

The target rate of return set by an organization, against which the return on investment of initiatives will be assessed. Also used as the discount rate to calculate net present value.

multi-criteria analysis

A technique applied to the appraisal of options (option appraisal) or an initiative (investment appraisal), or to rank initiatives (portfolio prioritization). Designed in part to address the issue of unreliable financial forecasts, it is based on assigning weights to relevant financial and non-financial criteria, and then scoring options or initiatives in terms of how well they perform against these criteria. Weighted scores are then summed, and can be used to rank options/initiatives including by means of a portfolio map or by dividing the total score by the cost of the option/initiative to calculate a score per £/$/€ invested.

portfolio

A grouping of an organization's projects and programmes. Portfolios can be managed at an organizational or functional level (APM, 2013).

pre-mortem

The pre-mortem (Klein, 1998) (which should be differentiated from post-mortem reviews that are undertaken after an initiative has failed) is a facilitated workshop undertaken at the start of an initiative. The initiative team is invited to imagine that the initiative has failed and the benefits haven't been realized, and use its creativity to explore the reasons why.

real option
An option based on the right to buy/sell a tangible asset, rather than a financial one. Can be used to incorporate the value of flexibility and uncertainty into investment appraisal.

senior responsible owner (SRO)
The individual who is accountable for an initiative meeting its objectives and optimizing benefits realization.

stage/phase gate review
Stage – a sub-division of the development phase of a project created to facilitate approval gates at suitable points in the lifecycle.

Gate – the point between phases, gates and/or tranches where a go/no-go decision can be made about the remainder of the work (APM, 2013).

start gate
An early stage review to ensure that the transition from strategy/policy to formally established change initiative is justified.

References

Andrew, J.P. and Sirkin, H.L. (2006) *Payback*, Harvard Business School Press, Boston, MA.

APM (2009) *Benefits Management – A Strategic Business Skill for All Seasons*. Available at: http://www.apm.org.uk/sites/default/files/APM_BenefitsManagement.pdf [Last accessed: 21 October 2014].

APM (June, 2011) *Delivering Benefits from Investments in Change: Creating Organisational Capability*. Available at: http://www.apm.org.uk/news/delivering-benefits-investment-change-creating-organisational-capability [Last accessed: 21 October 2014].

APM (2013) *Body of Knowledge*, 6th edition.

APM and CIMA (May, 2012) *Delivering the Prize – A Joint All-Ireland Study on Change Leadership and Benefits Realisation*. Available at: http://www.apm.org.uk/news/finance-minister-welcomes-all-ireland-report-change-leadership-and-benefits [Last accessed: 21 October 2014].

Asch, S. *Conformity experiments*. See http://en.wikipedia.org/wiki/Asch_conformity_experiments

Beer, M., Eisenstat, R.A. and Spector, B. (November–December 1990) Why Change Programs Don't Produce Change, *Harvard Business Review*, p. 158.

Cabinet Office (2006) *UK Approach to Benefits Realisation. Country report in support of the eGovernment Expert Meeting on the Cost and Benefit Analysis of e-Government*. Final version 0.11, 13 February 2006.

Dearing, A., Dilts, R. and Russell, J. (2002) *Alpha Leadership*, Wiley.

Flyvbjerg, B. (2006) From Nobel Prize to Project Management: Getting Risks Right. *Project Management Journal*, August 2006, pp. 5–15.

Flyvbjerg, B., Mette, K., Skamris, H. and Søren, L.B. (2005) How (In)accurate are Demand Forecasts in Public Works Projects?, *Journal of the American Planning Association*, Vol. 71, No. 2, Spring 2005.

Hastie, R. and Dawes, R.M. (2001) *Rational Choice in an Uncertain World*, Sage Publications.

HM Treasury (2003) *The Green Book – Appraisal and Evaluation in Central Government*. Available at: http://www.hm-treasury. gov.uk/data_greenbook_index.htm

Janis, I. (1972) *Victims of Groupthink*, Houghton-Mifflin, Boston.

Jenner, S. (2014) *Managing Benefits: Optimizing the Return from Investments*. APMG International.

Kahneman, D. (2011) *Thinking, Fast and Slow*, Allen Lane.

Kaplan, R.S. and Norton, D.P. (1996) *The Balanced Scorecard*, Harvard Business School Press.

Klein, G. (1998) *Sources of Power*, MIT Press.

Lin, C., Pervan, G. and McDermid, D. (2005) IS/IT Investment Evaluation and Benefits Realization Issues in Australia, *Journal of Research and Practice in Information Technology*, Vol. 37, No. 3, August 2005.

Lovallo, D. and Kahneman, D. (2003) Delusions of Success – How Optimism Undermines Executives' Decisions, *Harvard Business Review*, July 2003.

Marchand, D.A. (2004) Extracting the Business Value of IT: It is Usage, Not Just Deployment that Counts! *Capco Institute Journal of Financial Transformation*, Issue 11, August 2004, p. 127. Quoted in Jenner, S. (2010) *Transforming Government and Public Services – Realising Benefits through Project Portfolio Management*, Gower.

Moorhouse Consulting (2009a) *The Benefits of Organisational Change*. Copies of this and other reports referenced can be requested at: http://www.moorhouseconsulting.com/news-and-views/publications-and-articles

Moorhouse Consulting (2009b) *SRO Survey Results: Benchmarking Programme Sponsors' Attitudes*. Available at: http://www.moorhouseconsulting.com/site_assets/downloads/SRO_Survey_Results.pdf

NAO (2011) *Initiating Successful Projects*. Available at: http://www.nao.org.uk/report/nao-guide-initiating-successful-projects-3/

Peppard, J., Ward, J. and Daniel, E. (2007) Managing the Realization of Business Benefits from IT Investments, *MIS Quarterly Executive*, 6(1).

Pfeffer, J. and Sutton, R.I. (2000) *The Knowing–Doing Gap*, Harvard Business School Press.

Schaffer, R.H. and Thomson, H.A. (1992) Successful Change Programs Begin with Results, *Harvard Business Review*, January–February 1992, pp. 80–9. Available at: http://www.business.unr.edu/faculty/kuechler/788/successfulChangeProgramsBeginWithResults.pdf [Last accessed: 21 October 2014].

Surowiecki, J. (2004) *The Wisdom of Crowds*, Abacus, London.

Ward, J. (August, 2006) *Delivering Value from Information Systems and Technology Investments: Learning from Success*. A report of the results of an international survey of Benefits Management Practices in 2006. Available at: http://www.som.cranfield.ac.uk/som/dinamic-content/research/documents/deliveringvaluereport.pdf [Last accessed: 21 October 2014].

Ward, J., Daniel, E. and Peppard, J. (2008) Building Better Business Cases for IT Investments, *MIS Quarterly Executive*, 7(1).